This edition published by Parragon 2014

Parragon
Chartist House
15-17 Trim Street
Bath BA1 1HA, UK
www.parragon.com

ISBN 978-1-4454-5676-8
Printed in China

Nursery Rhymes

Bath • New York • Singapore • Hong Kong • Cologne • Delhi
Melbourne • Amsterdam • Johannesburg • Auckland • Shenzhen

Fee, Fi, Fo, Fum!

Fee, fi, fo, fum,
I smell the blood
Of an Englishman:
Be he alive or be he dead,
I'll grind his bones
To make my bread.

Roses Are Red

Roses are red,
Violets are blue,
Sugar is sweet
And so are you.

Mary, Mary

Mary, Mary, quite contrary,
How does your garden grow?
With silver bells and cockle shells
And pretty maids all in a row.

Hark! Hark!

Hark, hark,
The dogs do bark,
Beggars are coming to town:
Some in rags,
Some in tags,
And some in velvet gowns.

The Magpie

Magpie, magpie, flutter and flee,
Turn up your tail and good luck come to me.

Little Miss Muffet

Little Miss Muffet
Sat on a tuffet,
Eating her curds and whey;
There came a big spider,
Who sat down beside her,
And frightened Miss Muffet away.

Two Little Dicky Birds

Two little dicky birds sitting on a wall,
One named Peter, one named Paul.
Fly away, Peter!
Fly away, Paul!
Come back, Peter!
Come back, Paul!

Polly, Put the Kettle On

Polly, put the kettle on,
Polly, put the kettle on,
Polly, put the kettle on,
We'll all have tea.

Sukey, take it off again,
Sukey, take it off again,
Sukey, take it off again,
They've all gone away.

Little Robin Redbreast

Little Robin Redbreast
Sat upon a rail:
Niddle-noddle went his head!
Wiggle-waggle went his tail.

Hickory, Dickory, Dock

Hickory, dickory, dock,
The mouse ran up the clock,
The clock struck one,
The mouse ran down,
Hickory, dickory, dock.

The North Wind Doth Blow

The north wind doth blow,
And we shall have snow,
And what will poor Robin do then?
Poor thing!

He'll sit in a barn,
And to keep himself warm,
Will hide his head under his wing.
Poor thing!

Magpies

One for sorrow, two for joy,
Three for a girl, four for a boy,
Five for silver, six for gold,
Seven for a secret never to be told.

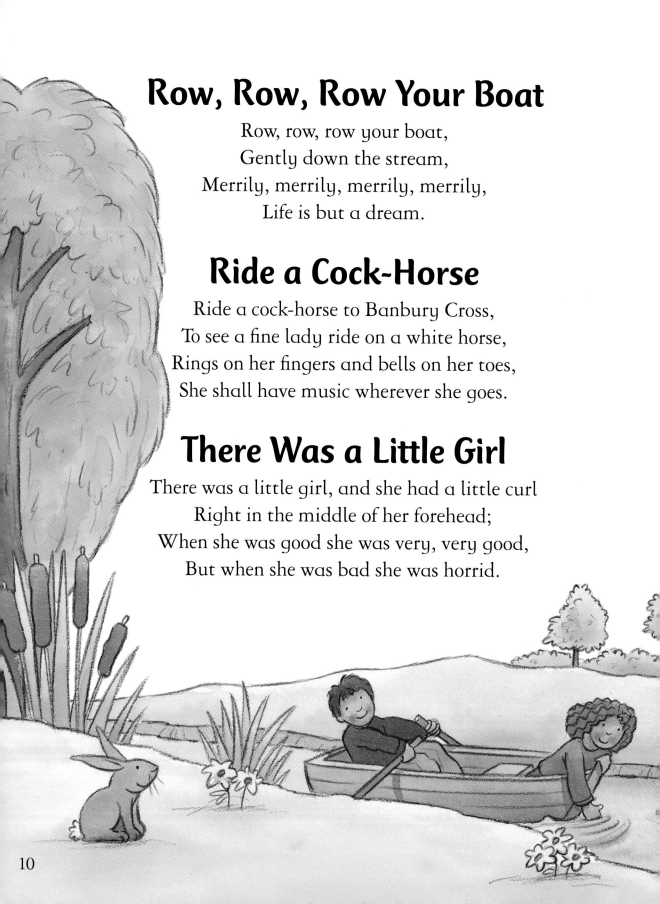

Row, Row, Row Your Boat

Row, row, row your boat,
Gently down the stream,
Merrily, merrily, merrily, merrily,
Life is but a dream.

Ride a Cock-Horse

Ride a cock-horse to Banbury Cross,
To see a fine lady ride on a white horse,
Rings on her fingers and bells on her toes,
She shall have music wherever she goes.

There Was a Little Girl

There was a little girl, and she had a little curl
Right in the middle of her forehead;
When she was good she was very, very good,
But when she was bad she was horrid.

See-saw, Margery Daw

See-saw, Margery Daw,
Johnny shall have a new master;
He shall have but a penny a day,
Because he can't work any faster.

Jack and Jill

Jack and Jill went up the hill
To fetch a pail of water;
Jack fell down and broke his crown,
And Jill came tumbling after.

Up Jack got, and home did trot
As fast as he could caper;
He went to bed, to mend his head,
With vinegar and brown paper.

Pat-a-Cake

Pat-a-cake, pat-a-cake, baker's man,
Bake me a cake as fast as you can.
Pat it and prick it and mark it with B,
And put it in the oven for Baby and me.

Ring-a-Ring o' Roses

Ring-a-ring o' roses,
A pocket full of posies,
A-tishoo! A-tishoo!
We all fall down!

Georgie Porgie

Georgie Porgie, pudding and pie,
Kissed the girls and made them cry;
When the boys came out to play
Georgie Porgie ran away.

Golden Slumbers

Golden slumbers kiss your eyes,
Smiles await you when you rise;
Sleep, pretty baby, do not cry,
And I will sing a lullaby.

Way Down Yonder in the Maple Swamp

Way down yonder in the maple swamp
The wild geese gather and the ganders honk;
The mares kick up and the ponies prance;
The old sow whistles and the little pigs dance.

Mrs Hen

Chook, chook, chook, chook, chook,
Good morning, Mrs Hen.
How many chickens have you got?
Madam, I've got ten.
Four of them are yellow,
And four of them are brown,
And two of them are speckled red,
The nicest in the town.

Little Boy Blue

Little Boy Blue, come blow your horn,
The sheep's in the meadow,
The cow's in the corn.
Where is the boy who looks after the sheep?
He's under a haycock fast asleep.
Will you wake him?
No, not I,
For if I do he's sure to cry.

Humpty Dumpty

Humpty Dumpty sat on a wall,
Humpty Dumpty had a great fall;
All the king's horses and all the king's men
Couldn't put Humpty together again.

Doctor Foster

Doctor Foster
Went to Gloucester
In a shower of rain;
He stepped in a puddle,
Right up to his middle,
And never went there again!

Oranges and Lemons

Oranges and lemons,
Say the bells of St Clements.
I owe you five farthings,
Say the bells of St Martins.
When will you pay me?
Say the bells of Old Bailey.
When I grow rich,
Say the bells of Shoreditch.

Daffy-Down-Dilly

Daffy-Down-Dilly
Has come up to town
In a yellow petticoat
And a green gown.

Star Light, Star Bright

Star light, star bright,
First star I see tonight,
I wish I may, I wish I might,
Have the wish I wish tonight.

Jack Be Nimble

Jack be nimble,
And Jack be quick:
And Jack jump over
The candlestick.

Mary, Mary, Quite Contrary

Mary, Mary, quite contrary,
How does your garden grow?
With silver bells and cockle shells,
And pretty maids all in a row.

Lucy Locket

Lucy Locket lost her pocket,
Kitty Fisher found it.
Not a penny was there in it,
Only ribbon round it.

A Sailor Went to Sea

A sailor went to sea, sea, sea,
To see what he could see, see, see,
But all that he could see, see, see,
Was the bottom of the deep blue sea, sea, sea.

This Little Piggy

This little piggy went to market,
This little piggy stayed at home,
This little piggy had roast beef,
This little piggy had none,
And this little piggy cried
Wee-wee-wee-wee-wee!
All the way home.

Bob Robin

Little Bob Robin,
Where do you live?
Up in yonder wood, sir,
On a hazel twig.

One, Two, Three, Four, Five

One, two, three, four, five,
Once I caught a fish alive.
Six, seven, eight, nine, ten,
Then I let it go again.

Why did you let it go?
Because it bit my finger so.
Which finger did it bite?
This little finger on my right.

There Was a Crooked Man

There was a crooked man, and he went a crooked mile,
He found a crooked sixpence against a crooked stile;
He bought a crooked cat, which caught a crooked mouse,
And they all lived together in a little crooked house.

Baa, Baa, Black Sheep

Baa, baa, black sheep, have you any wool?
Yes, sir, yes, sir, three bags full;
One for the master, one for the dame,
And one for the little boy that lives down the lane.

I Hear Thunder

I hear thunder, I hear thunder,
Hark! don't you? Hark! don't you?
Pitter, patter raindrops, pitter, patter raindrops,
I'm wet through, I'm wet through.

Pop Goes the Weasel

Half a pound of tuppenny rice,
Half a pound of treacle.
That's the way the money goes,
Pop! goes the weasel.

Hot Cross Buns

Hot cross buns!
Hot cross buns!
One-a-penny, two-a-penny,
Hot cross buns!
If you have no daughters,
Give them to your sons,
One-a-penny, two-a-penny,
Hot cross buns!

Pease Pudding Hot

Pease pudding hot, pease pudding cold,
Pease pudding in the pot – nine days old.
Some like it hot, some like it cold,
Some like it in the pot – nine days old!

Round and Round the Garden

Round and round the garden,
Like a teddy bear.
One step, two steps,
Tickly under there!

The Grand Old Duke of York

The grand old Duke of York,
He had ten thousand men,
He marched them up to the top of the hill,
And he marched them down again.

When they were up, they were up,
And when they were down, they were down,
And when they were only half way up,
They were neither up nor down.

Oats and Beans

Oats and beans and barley grow,
Oats and beans and barley grow,
Do you or I or anyone know,
How oats and beans and barley grow?

First the farmer sows his seeds,
Then he stands and takes his ease,
Stamps his feet and claps his hands,
Turns around to view the land.

Hey Diddle Diddle

Hey diddle diddle,
The cat and the fiddle,
The cow jumped over the moon.
The little dog laughed to see such fun,
And the dish ran away with the spoon.

Jack Sprat

Jack Sprat could eat no fat,
His wife could eat no lean,
And so between the two of them
They licked the platter clean.

Rub-a-Dub Dub

Rub-a-dub dub, three men in a tub,
And who do you think they be?
The butcher, the baker, the candle-stick maker,
Turn them out knaves all three.

The Queen of Hearts

The Queen of Hearts, she made some tarts,
All on a summer's day;
The Knave of Hearts, he stole the tarts,
And took them clean away.
The King of Hearts called for the tarts,
And beat the Knave full sore;
The Knave of Hearts brought back the tarts,
And vowed he'd steal no more.

Mary Had a Little Lamb

Mary had a little lamb,
Its fleece was white as snow,
And everywhere that Mary went,
The lamb was sure to go.

It followed her to school one day,
Which was against the rule;
It made the children laugh and play,
To see a lamb at school.

Little Bo-Peep

Little Bo-Peep has lost her sheep,
And doesn't know where to find them;
Leave them alone,
And they'll come home,
Wagging their tails behind them.

Little Jack Horner

Little Jack Horner,
Sat in a corner,
Eating a Christmas pie.
He put in his thumb,
And pulled out a plum,
And said, "What a good boy am I!"

Old King Cole

Old King Cole was a merry old soul,
And a merry old soul was he;
He called for his pipe, and he called for his bowl,
And he called for his fiddlers three.

Little Blue Ben

Little Blue Ben, who lives in the glen,
Keeps a blue cat and one blue hen,
Which lays of blue eggs a score and ten;
Where shall I find the little Blue Ben?

Hickory, Dickory, Dock

Hickory, dickory, dock,
The mouse ran up the clock.
The clock struck one,
The mouse ran down,
Hickory, dickory, dock.

One, Two, Buckle my Shoe

One, two, buckle my shoe,
Three, four, knock at the door;
Five, six, pick up sticks;
Seven, eight, lay them straight;
Nine, ten, a big fat hen;
Eleven, twelve, dig and delve;
Thirteen, fourteen, maids a-courting;
Fifteen, sixteen, maids in the kitchen;
Seventeen, eighteen, maids in waiting;
Nineteen, twenty, my plate's empty!

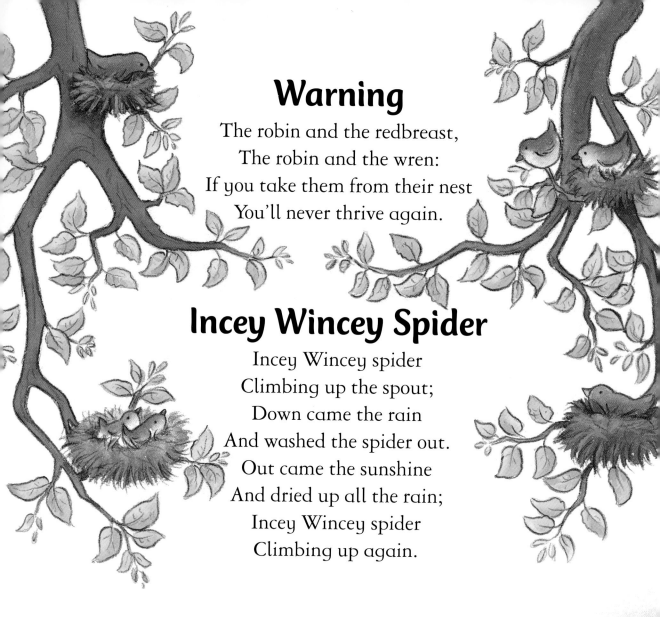

Warning

The robin and the redbreast,
The robin and the wren:
If you take them from their nest
You'll never thrive again.

Incey Wincey Spider

Incey Wincey spider
Climbing up the spout;
Down came the rain
And washed the spider out.
Out came the sunshine
And dried up all the rain;
Incey Wincey spider
Climbing up again.

I'm a Little Teapot

I'm a little teapot, short and stout,
Here's my handle, here's my spout.
When I get my steam up hear me shout,
Tip me up and pour me out!

Hush-a-bye, Baby

Hush-a-bye, baby, on the tree-top,
When the wind blows the cradle will rock;
When the bough breaks the cradle will fall,
Down will come baby, cradle and all.

Old Mother Goose

Old Mother Goose,
When she wanted to wander,
Would ride through the air
On a very fine gander.

Wee Willie Winkie

Wee Willie Winkie runs through the town,
Upstairs and downstairs in his nightgown,
Peeping through the keyhole, crying through the lock,
"Are the children in their beds? It's past eight o'clock!"

It's Raining, It's Pouring

It's raining, it's pouring,
The old man is snoring;
He went to bed and bumped his head
And couldn't get up in the morning.

Rain, Rain, Go Away

Rain, rain,
Go away,
Come again
Another day.

The Wind

Who has seen the wind? Neither I nor you;
But when the leaves hang trembling
The wind is passing through.

Who has seen the wind? Neither you nor I;
But when the trees bow down their heads
The wind is passing by.

Three Blind Mice

Three blind mice, three blind mice!
See how they run, see how they run!
They all ran after the farmer's wife,
Who cut off their tails with a carving-knife,
Did ever you see such a thing in your life,
As three blind mice?

Tom, Tom, the Piper's Son

Tom, Tom, the piper's son,
Stole a pig and away he ran.
The pig was eat, and Tom was beat,
And Tom went roaring down the street.

Lavender's Blue

Lavender's blue, dilly, dilly,
Lavender's green;
When I am king, dilly, dilly,
You shall be queen.